A Football Goalpost Killed My Son

Jonathan Smith 1979 - 1991

By Brenda Smith

A Football Goalpost Killed My Son

Published by:
Chipmunkapublishing
PO Box 6872
Brentwood
Essex
CM13 1ZT
United Kingdom

http://www.chipmunkapublishing.com

A Football Goalpost Killed My Son

Jonathan died on Sunday the 13th of January after an unsafe goalpost fell on him and ruptured his heart. That day was the worst day of my life and nothing can put into words the loss that all my family has felt. At the time it was reported to be a tragic accident but it has turned out that is was a needless unnecessary preventable death.

I was to find myself discovering more about football goalposts then I ever thought possible. I have leaflets, diagrams, photographs and booklets on them relating to assembly, fixing use, storage, you name it I have researched it.

Over the next seventeen years I have fought mainly on my own, to get legislation in place so that everyone playing football is safe.

I have already written about the subject in my first book – **Good Night Jonathan Good Morning Laura – also published by Chipmunka Publications**, but that was more about my feelings than the actual details of my campaign. Also the book only touched on the subject and is more about bringing up a child with complex special needs.

This book contains all aspects of my campaign and the fight I have had to keep the dangers of unsafe goals in the public eye. It contains all copies of relevant support, a summary of the letters I have written, letters of support I have received and newspaper cuttings of my campaign.

I have decided to write this as I am still disappointed after seventeen years that I have to hear of new deaths and accidents from unsafe goalposts. Only the week before I had started to write this, on the 12th February 2008, 6 days before my last meeting with The Football Association, a goalkeeper was killed during a football game with friends when goalposts collapsed and crushed him.

A Football Goalpost Killed My Son

The 37 year old man from Labin in Croatia was warming up when the accident happened. He dived to save the ball but missed and got entangled in the net. As he fell, he pulled the iron goalpost with him and it struck him on the head and spine, killing him instantly.

This news makes me so sad to think that I have wasted the last seventeen years, will no one listen and act to prevent these needless deaths.

On this page photographs of the goals that killed Jonathan taken by the Health and Safety Executive the day after he died.

A Football Goalpost Killed My Son

Although the Football Association has been supportive, I can't achieve legislation on my own. As they are the football governing body in this country, people would take notice of them and not me. **The message about unsafe goalposts should reach the rest of the world.**

First correspondence with Football Association 31st May 1991.

In August of the same year, I traveled up to London to meet Graham Kelly, the then Chief Executive of the Football Association, to discuss goalpost safety , when I was 8 months pregnant, but saw some one else, as he apparently was too busy to see me.

August 1991, Jonathan's accident highlighted in the grounds man's official journal.

The goalposts that killed Jonathan were made from heavy metal tubing, lighter tubing forming the rear supports – it took 4 adults to lift these goal frames into place.

The goal posts were not originally free standing and consisted of 2 posts and a cross bar, the back supports being added later, allowing the goal frames to be free standing and portable. The goals were not manufactured by a reputable firm but by a friend of the football club who worked for a welding company and who had volunteered to make them, to save money. They were also not made to any specific FA size or requirement. **They were just scaffold poles welded together, not fixed down, and weighed 200lbs.**

The Health and safety Executive at the time issued Improvement notices to the football club management committee requiring that they institute a safer system of work in connection with the use of all portable goalposts. Also that the ones that had killed Jonathan had not been adequately secured. **Health and Safety representative also found a number of pegs suitable for use with the goalposts lying in a shed adjacent to the stored posts.**

I found out much later that one Coroner had written to another about similar goal post fatalities, 'for what it may be worth, I did make a report to the Health and Safety Executive and to the local authority under rule 43. The Health and Safety, 'ducked out' of doing anything, except to forward my letter to the Executive Headquarters.'

You may all now understand the reasons I have kept on fighting to make football a safer game for children to enjoy, and family and friends to watch.

A Football Goalpost Killed My Son

GOALPOST ACCIDENT KILLS BOY

A WITHAM schoolboy footballer died when goalposts toppled onto him as his mother watched from a nearby clubhouse.

Jonathan Smith, 11, had been swinging from the crossbar of the six-foot-high goal frame.

The freak accident happened at the Stony Stratford Town Football Club in Milton Keynes, where Jonathan and his friends from Witham Under-12s Valley Green Football Club were due to play an away match.

His mother, Brenda, saw the accident from the clubhouse. She said today she believed he had died almost instantly from a broken neck.

Mrs Smith and his father, Peter, had both travelled by coach from Witham with the team for the match.

She said: " I saw the goalpost fall and just knew it was him. Everyone did all they could to save him."

She added: " He loved football. He was always out practising."

She praised those who attempted to save Jonathan's life immediately after the accident.

Nurse Pat Ohean, a parent of one of the Witham boys, and fireman Pete Smith, the Valley Green chairman, gave mouth-to-mouth resuscita[tion] [a]nd emergency services w[ere] immediately called.

Manager Gary Oates said [Jo]nathan, who joined the clu[b in] August, was playing with friends before the match.

The teams had been wai[ting] for the pitch to thaw after [the] frost before starting the gam[e,] part of the East Anglia Sun[day] Youth Cup competition — the boys were playing near [a] goalpost on the way to wal[king] back to the clubhouse.

A pupil at Rickstones Sc[hool,] Witham, Jonathan form[erly] went to the town's Templars [jun]ior and infant schools.

An inquest is due to be op[ened] at Milton Keynes tomorrow.

Club desolated

MANAGER of the Valley Green Under-12s, Gary Oates, said the club was shocked and desolated by Jonathan's death.

" I have been involved in football for more than 20 years and have never known anything like this to happen before," said Mr Oates.

Mr Oates said he had cancelled future games indefinitely.

" Jonathan always gave 100 per cent and never missed a training session," he said.

• Jonathan — pictured in football [g]ear last year.

A Football Goalpost Killed My Son

Soccer boy is mourned

by
EVE SWEETING

HUNDREDS of mourners packed St Nicolas Church in Witham for the funeral of 11-year-old **Jonathan Smith** who died in a freak accident on a football pitch.

West Ham international player Stuart Slater, who is in the England Under 21 first team, and West Ham first team coach Ronnie Boyce were among those present.

Jonathan, of Tees Close, Witham, was a keen West Ham supporter.

In his address, the vicar of Witham, the Rev Desmond Sherlock, said no-one was to blame for the tragic accident which "comes out of the blue."

He praised Witham Valley Green Football Club chairman Pete Smith and nurse Pat Ohene, mother of one of the boys in the team who tried desperately to save Jonathan's life.

Jonathan died after a mobile training goal frame toppled on top of him. He had been swinging from the crossbar of the six foot high frame.

The accident happened at the Stony Stratford Town Football Club in Milton Keynes where Jonathan and his team mates in the Under 12s Valley Green club were due to play an away match.

Valley Green is now setting up a trust fund in Jonathan's name for youngsters who are injured in sport and need special treatment.

Already hundreds of pounds have been collected and anyone who would like to donate to the fund is asked to ring club chairman Pete Smith on Witham 511517 or the under 12s team manager Gary Oates on Witham 516412.

The service started with the psalm The Lord is My Shepherd and included the hymn All Things Bright and Beautiful.

Jonathan's favourite tunes — Bubbles and the Stevie Wonder song I Just Called To Say I Love You — were played.

The coffin was covered in flowers and on top were Jonathan's football boots.

His mother Brenda said she chose the Stevie Wonder song because Jonathan used to say "I love you" to her when he rang her up.

Both she and Jonathan's father Peter said they wanted to thank the many people who have sent them messages of sympathy. They have received more than 100 cards and letters.

● People who would like to contribute to The Jonathan Smith Memorial Trust can pay the money through The Halifax Building Society or through Roger Hart Solicitors in Guithavon Street, Witham.

Club tribute to Jonathan

JONATHAN'S team manager, Gary Oates, paid tribute to his young player.

He said: "Jonathan had a vast appetite for the game and would never miss a training session.

"He would work hard to master a skill he might have originally found difficult.

"Nothing was going to beat Jonathan. He would be continually practising even outside official training sessions.

"Jonathan had become an integral part of the squad and during any game could be relied upon to give 100 per cent at all times.

"During a league cup game when all others around him were missing goal-scoring chances, the one that fell to Jonathan he calmly put away to send us winners into the next round.

"It will be extremely difficult to replace Jonathan's enthusiasm and eagerness to play football and he will be sorely missed by myself, his team mates and everybody at the club."

A Football Goalpost Killed My Son

THE FOOTBALL ASSOCIATION
LIMITED
Founded 1863

Patron: HER MAJESTY THE QUEEN
President: H.R.H. THE DUKE OF KENT
Chairman: F. A. MILLICHIP

Chief Executive:
R. H. G. KELLY FCIS

Phone: 071-402 7151/071-262 4542
Telex: 261110
Facsimile: 071-402 0486

16 LANCASTER GATE, LONDON W2 3LW

Our Ref: RHGK/DB/7039   *Your Ref:*

31st May 1991

Dear Mrs. Smith,

Thank you for your letter.

We had read about the accident in the national press and received detailed information very soon afterwards from the Assistant Director (Health) at the Borough of Milton Keynes.

The Executive Committee of The Football Association considered the matter at its next meeting. It was later decided that the next issue of "FA News", a publication which is sent free of charge to Club and County Association officials, would include some important recommendations.

The first was that the practice of using goalposts for warming up or fooling around should be actively discouraged, especially amongst young players.

Secondly, clubs were to be informed of the absolute need to ensure that goalposts are securely anchored and that the state of goalposts and crossbars, together with any stanchions, are regularly monitored.

We cannot begin to imagine what you as parents have been through since that tragic day. We accept that accidents of this nature are thankfully rare and we sincerely hope that, through our published recommendations to members, the likelihood of something similar happening in the future will be reduced.

Yours sincerely,

R.H.G. Kelly

A Football Goalpost Killed My Son

HOUSE OF COMMONS
LONDON SW1A 0AA

13 June 1991.

Dear Mrs. Smith,

Thank you for your letter of 11th June, following on from your conversation with my Secretary. Needless to say I was desperately sorry to hear about the tragic death of your son Jonathan and offer you and your family my heartfelt sympathy.

I greatly admire your efforts to ensure that other families do not have to suffer in the same way and I myself would obviously want to see anything possible done to prevent such a tragedy being repeated.

I am therefore raising this with the Minister for Sport and will, of course, come back to you when I hear from him.

With sympathetic good wishes.

Yours sincerely,

Tony Newton

A Football Goalpost Killed My Son

THE DEPARTMENT OF EDUCATION AND SCIENCE   RA/0066/1019

ELIZABETH HOUSE YORK ROAD LONDON SE1 7PH
TELEPHONE 071-934 9000

ROBERT ATKINS MP
Minister for Sport

The Rt Hon Tony Newton OBE MP
House of Commons
London
SW1A 0AA

12 AUG 1991

Dear Tony,

Thank you for your letter of 13 June with which you enclosed copies of correspondence sent to you by your constituent Mrs Brenda Smith of 12 Tees Close, Witham about the tragic death of her son Jonathan. Please pass on my sincerest condolences to Mr & Mrs Smith.

Jonathan's tragic accident and the others mentioned in the correspondence you sent to me have resulted in a great deal of concern and action has been taken by several influential bodies to warn potential users of free standing goal posts of their dangers and to give advice on how to avoid similar accidents in the future. As you are aware the Football Association included an item in the most recent issue of its official bulletin - FA News - which is distributed widely to clubs and county football associations. The FA have advised clubs that they should be aware of the absolute need to ensure that goalposts are securely anchored and that the condition of the whole assembly should be regularly monitored. They have also told clubs that they should actively discourage players from climbing onto goalposts.

The Institute of Groundsmanship, the professional body for groundsmen, have also highlighted the case in their official journal, the Groundsman, and given practical advice on how free standing goalposts can be made more stable. They suggest that a four foot length of steel, bent to the shape of a hairpin, should be hammered into the ground with one prong on either side of the back bar to act as an anchor thus preventing the whole structure from toppling forward. We will be asking the Football Association to consider bringing to the attention of clubs the Institute of Groundmanship's advice.

So far as current legislation is concerned I understand that under the Health and Safety at Work Act 1974 those who have

3

DES

A Football Goalpost Killed My Son

control of premises made available for use by others have a duty
to take reasonable measures to ensure the safety of any equipment
they provide for use on those premises. The duty does not however
extend to equipment provided by the users themselves or another
party.

I quite appreciate that however useful, advice from the FA
and the Institute of Groundsmanship to prevent future accidents
is not sufficient, and current legislation does not address the
problem of free standing goalposts provided by the clubs
themselves. You and Mr & Mrs Smith will therefore be interested
to know that CEN (the European Standards Organisation) is
currently working on a standard specifically for goalposts,
including the free standing type. The standard will lay down
safety requirements for the construction and installation of
goalposts. It will provide manufactures of goalposts, those who
use them and those responsible for their installation with clear
guidance on what steps should be taken to ensure that they are
safe. It is hoped that the standard will be published before the
end of 1992. We will be drawing the attention of the FA and the
Institute of Groundsmanship to the proposed standard in order
that they can give publicity to it when it is finalised.

Yours etc.

Michael Fallon

ROBERT ATKINS
pp

11

A Football Goalpost Killed My Son

In between all the letter writing and research that I did at the time, without the internet as seventeen years ago it was not widely available as it is now. I found out I was pregnant which was such a shock; I thought my family was complete. Also we attended the Coroner's inquest which was very traumatic as we relived the events of Jonathan's death.

The Coroner said, 'As a result of the death of Jonathan, the message has gone far and wide that no longer should these free standing goalposts be unsecured' for the very reason you see in this case.'

A Football Goalpost Killed My Son

Sad lessons from soccer lad's death

by
VICTORIA MILES

AN inquest jury has returned a verdict of accidental death after a Witham boy died in a freak football pitch accident.

Jonathan Smith, 11, of Tees Close, Witham, died when a goalpost toppled onto him after he had been swinging on the crossbar before an under-12s match.

The inquest heard that the free-standing goalpost which toppled on top of Jonathan was not secured to the ground — although some football clubs with similar posts pegged them down as a safety precaution.

North Bucks coroner Rodney Corner said: " Swinging on goals, in a nutshell, you don't do. But you are dealing with a boy of 11 and boys of 11 do these things."

Mr Corner said it was often in tragic circumstances when certain dangers come to light in such a " stark fashion."

He added: " As a result of the death of Jonathan the message has gone out far and wide that no longer should these free-standing goal posts be unsecured, for the very reason you see in this case."

RUPTURED

The inquest at Milton Keynes yesterday heard that the accident happened when Witham under-12s Valley Green football club went to Stony Stratford to play in an East Anglian Sunday Youth Cup game.

Pathologist Doctor Khin Lwin said Jonathan died due to the front wall of his heart being ruptured.

She said the injury was consistant with scaffolding falling on someone's chest.

Kim Bennett, environmental health officer for Milton Keynes Borough Council, said after writing to the Football Association about the incident it had decided to issue guidelines and advice about the use of mobile goal posts.

A police statement claimed that when the Witham football team first arrived at the football ground about five boys were seen swinging from the cross bar before Jonathan began swinging on it."

• Jonathan Smith — accidental death verdict.

21-3-91

After the inquest we concentrated on getting our lives back together as a family. At this time we all left the house together and arrived home at the same time as none of us wanted to be on our own.

Emma our daughter was only thirteen when Jonathan died and had to grow up overnight. She helped her dad and me through our grief by just being an excellent teenager and wonderful daughter. She was delighted about the baby which was due in September, 9 months after the death of a much loved son.

Laura was born on 30th September 1991 and brought so much peace and joy to not only Peter, Emma and I but also to all our family and friends. You can never replace a child but Laura

13

certainly gave us something to focus on and help our grief.

In January 1992 I approached That's Life the consumer television programme and the TV campaigner Esther Rantzen, which was very popular, and was delighted when they said that they would do a piece about goalpost safety. Jonathan's accident was featured on the programme. As a result Esther said, 'The reaction has been enormous, we have heard from hundreds of people, including football clubs and councils.'

A Football Goalpost Killed My Son

Catching up on campaign success. Esther Rantzen meets the Smiths — Peter, Brenda and baby Laura.   Picture: Dave Barker.

That's Life backing for goalpost safety

ESTHER Rantzen praised the courage of football tragedy boy parents Brenda and Peter Smith when she met them in Witham on Thursday.

The TV campaigner came to Witham to present life saving awards to Howbridge Junior School.

She and That's Life producer Donna Taberer spoke to the Smiths about reaction to the recent That's Life programme which featured the tragedy of their son Jonathan's death.

Jonathan, 11, of Tees Close, Witham, died just over a year ago when goalposts he was swinging on toppled onto him, rupturing his heart.

Ever since his parents Brenda and Peter Smith have been fighting a campaign to get legislation on the pegging of mobile goalposts.

That's Life, which has millions of viewers, is backing the campaign.

Esther Rantzen told Mr and Mrs Smith on Thursday how much she admired their courage in being featured in the programme. "The reaction has been enormous, we have heard from hundreds of people, including football clubs and councils" she said.

Since the programme the That's Life team has heard of another death and many more accidents involving unsecured mobile goalposts.

Hundreds of parents, football clubs and councils, concerned about the potential dangers of freestanding goalposts, have contacted That's Life asking for fact sheets on safety anchors.

The fact sheet says problems can arise with all types and sizes of mobile goalposts, whether they are home-made or manufactured. On hard surfaces the goalposts should either be weighted down or chained up.

A Football Goalpost Killed My Son

The years after I first started campaigning were then taken up by my new baby daughter Laura as we found out that she had complex special needs, as mentioned on my first page, I have written a book about the day to day life with a child with such needs.

This didn't stop me still making comments to the press every time there was an incident concerning football goalposts, I wish now I could have done more at the time and maybe some of the children that have died would still be here.

FA repeats safety advice

THE Football Association has renewed its safety advice on mobile goalposts in the light of the latest tragedy.

But the attempt to answer the concern of safety campaigners falls short of their demands for new laws.

The FA directive on the potentially deadly posts, first produced in June, was reiterated by the sports ruling body after a 13-year-old Lancashire schoolboy died.

Mobile five-a-side goalposts fell on Wayne Turner at a sports centre.

PEGGING

Four years ago Jonathan Smith, 11, of Tees Close, Witham, died in similar circumstances.

He suffered a ruptured heart and ever since parents Brenda and Peter have been campaigning for legislation to make the pegging of mobile goalposts compulsory.

A spokeswoman for the FA said it recommends all posts should be stable, wherever possible either six or eight feet in height, and cones and markers used in place of posts that are any smaller.

At last the Football Association are listening!!!!!!!!!!!

A Football Goalpost Killed My Son

Below press cuttings from a goalpost death only 20 miles from where I live, also a nasty accident involving unsafe goalposts which could have been prevented if safety measures were law.

by EVE SWEETING and JON WHITE

Mother of goalposts death boy devastated by new tragedy

THE mother of a boy who died when portable goalposts collapsed on him said today she was devastated to find a similar tragedy had happened – four years after she campaigned for safety measures.

Jonathan Smith, 11, of Tees Close, Witham, died in 1991 from a ruptured heart.

His parents, Brenda and Peter Smith, campaigned for legislation to make the pegging of mobile goal posts compulsory. Now there has been another tragedy. Earlier this week 13-year-old schoolboy Wayne Turner died after a set of mobile five-a-side football goalposts collapsed on him after he had been seen swinging on the cross-bar.

He was dead on arrival at hospital and had suffered a fractured skull.

Mrs Smith said: "It is a nightmare to hear of yet another tragedy. Since Jonathan died we have heard of at least three other similar deaths. Where will it all end?

"We campaigned because we did not want what happened to Jonathan to happen to another child and devastate another family. And yet it is still going on. How many more people must die before something is done?"

THE Football Association today said it will make an international bid to alter the safety rules governing mobile goalposts.

The FA's announcement follows the news that a young footballer whose arm was broken when a goalpost fell on top of him has been awarded £5,500 damages by Colchester County Court.

An FA spokesman said it plans to put forward a recommendation to the International Football Board that the rules of the game should be changed to say that goalposts should be securely anchored to the ground.

If this is accepted, all ga-

by EVE SWEETING and VINCE ELLIS

mes will be covered by the ruling.

Yesterday's hearing was told how Ben Etheridge was playing in goal at a practice for Woodham Radars under-14s in South Woodham Ferrers.

Mr Etheridge, now 18, of Ornesby Chine, South Woodham Ferrers, had just tried to save a shot when the goal was brushed by another player and it toppled on to his arm, the court heard.

He told the court he can now only partially move his right arm.

Mr Etheridge accused brothers Trevor and Tony Jones, who managed and coached the team, of being negligent and failing to secure a goalpost safely in August 1988.

The Joneses denied negligence but the case was found proved at Colchester County Court yesterday.

● Witham schoolboy Jonathan Smith died in 1991, aged 11, after goalposts on which he was swinging toppled on to him.

Jonathan's father Peter today said he welcomed the FA's safety move, but it was "not before time".

A Football Goalpost Killed My Son

Still more deaths and injuries, as my comment on the above first press cutting says, 'We campaigned because we did not want what happened to Jonathan to happen to another family. And yet it is still going on. How many more must die before something is done?'

Unexpectedly on the 11th August 1997 I received a letter from Stony Stratford Town Football Club, the club where Jonathan had died. They informed me that a plaque had been erected in Jonathan's name. Mixed feelings and emotions again, but a nice gesture from the club.

A Football Goalpost Killed My Son

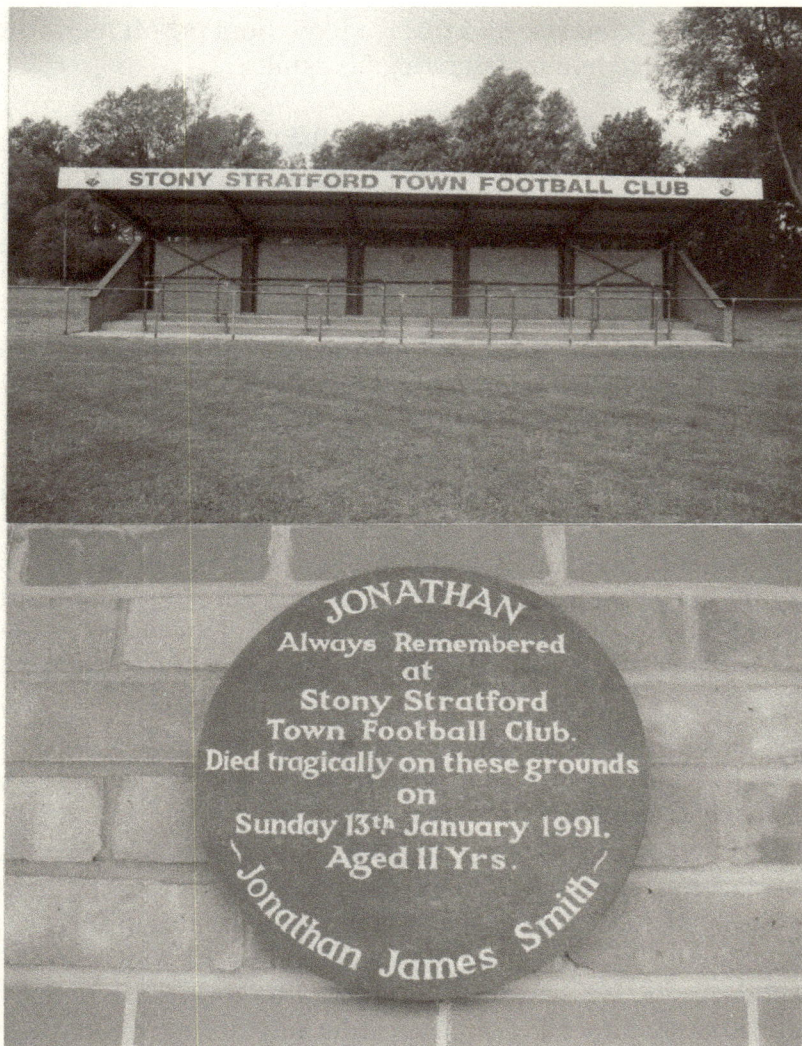

Sadly in July 1999 another child was killed, his name was Jack Sheerin he was 7 years old, he died when a movable goalpost fell on his head. He had been attending a holiday training session at Thornhill Football Club, near Dewsbury, West Yorkshire. The

A Football Goalpost Killed My Son

inquest in Bradford was told that the blow from the 6ft high steel-tubed post killed him by fracturing his skull.

It fell as up to four children swung on the posts and crossbar. The posts had holes to which securing pegs could be fixed, but they had not been used because nets were not being attached.
The police said that 8 other children, aged between 2 and 13, had been killed in similar accidents between 1986 and 1996. 4 children had also been injured between 1990 and 1994. Safety guidelines had been issued by the FA in 1991 after the death of an 11 year old (Jonathan), but he said that there was still a need for clarity over who was responsible for goalpost safety.

The coroner recorded a verdict of accidental death, as was in Jonathan's case. He added that unless goalposts are adequately anchored at the back, they will fall forward. Kids will be kids and play on things. Some form of regulation is necessary, not just to prevent them playing – that can only be done by someone seeing them – but there's got to be an overall regulation to prevent it.

He said also, 'he was using his powers under 1984 Coroner's Rules to report the matter to the Department of Education.' The FA declined to make a detailed comment until it had seen the full text of the coroner's comments, but a spokesman said: 'The FA has undertaken an awareness campaign on promoting good practice with regards to goalpost safety to every area of the game. In addition, we continue to work closely with goalpost manufacturers. We have also introduced an awareness initiative on the issue into all FA coach education courses, and have circulated information through a number of football magazines aimed at people involved with running football at local level.'

When I heard about Jack's death I was again contacted by the media, and this time I decided that I would contact the family and tell them about my campaign.
It was one of the hardest phone calls I have ever made. After the initial tearful chat we decided to join forces and campaign together, this would then put far more pressure on the government

A Football Goalpost Killed My Son

and the Football Association to stop these needless deaths happening.

Between us we obtained massive media coverage and had meetings with the Sport's Minister Kate Hoey and the Football Association. We also had television interviews on local television, BBC news, Sky news as well as articles in magazines.

Susan Sheerin, (Jack's mother) and I spoke regularly on the phone and got on really well she became a friend. We exchanged our thoughts and spoke often about Jonathan and Jack.
Her feelings were the same as mine in that The FA and the government should sit down and talk to produce guidelines and eventually legislation.
The FA need to be involved as they are the organization that the football teams are governed by. We both were aware that although guidelines had been sent to clubs sometimes they are not seen by the people that need to see them and are then filed away. A circular was issued after Jack died but how many clubs took notice of it! As Susan once said to me, 'if something had happened, if only someone had listened to me when Jonathan died, perhaps Jack would still be here today.' These conversations always upset us both, but we still needed to carry on. Unless you have lost a child the trauma is unexplainable and in Jonathan's and Jack's deaths they could so easily have been prevented.

Other thoughts we had were that, if a football player gets fined and does not pay, the club then gets fined and then sometimes bans are put in place. So the same should be for goalposts the club should be fined and then banned if they do not reach the required standard. Local Environmental Health Officer to enforce – recommendations not enough.

Football coaches and trainers made aware of the dangers, local authorities, sports centres, and schools all to be made aware.

- Portable goals that can be packed away only cost £150 and are easy to assemble and pack away.

A Football Goalpost Killed My Son

- BSI to set a standard that clubs would have to use.
- Large publicity campaign needed to show the dangers.
- Write to manufacturers who make both aluminium and metal posts.
- Maybe a large poster campaign with Jonathan and Jack featured on it, like the transport campaign for drink driving; it would have more of an impact with real people.

On the next few pages there is a sample of press cuttings from the campaign.

GAZETTE GOALPOST CAMPAIGN
STOP THESE NEEDLESS DEATHS

Top boss George backs our fight

by MATT PLUMMER

TOTTENHAM Hotspur manager George Graham has given the Gazette's goalpost campaign his seal of approval.

The former Arsenal, Manchester United and Scotland hero is the latest personality to back our drive for compulsory safety laws.

Witham mum Brenda Smith – whose son Jonathan died when unsecured posts fell on him – helped us launch the campaign following the recent death of Manchester United fan Jack Sheerin.

The seven-year-old was killed when a steel post toppled over during a football coaching session near his home in Dewsbury, West Yorkshire.

Mr Graham, ex-manager of Leeds United, said: "This is extremely sad news and it's crucial such a tragic event must not be allowed to happen again.

"All over the country youngsters who love their football will be playing in the same innocent way young Jack and Jonathan did and they must be protected.

"As a child, goalposts were always a major attraction to me and my friends and that understandable magnetism is still evident in the local parks today.

"We must ensure their safety to safeguard our children.

"I have no hesitation in applauding and backing the Gazette's initiative in the hope some light can be found in this darkness."

Mr Graham joins the Football Association, the influential Football Supporter's Association, and Braintree MP Alan Hurst in our fight for a change in current safety legislation.

● George Graham – safe plea.

A Football Goalpost Killed My Son

Action needed on mobile posts

All the news from Witham with EVE SWEETING

FIRST FOR WITHAM NEWS

LAST week a boy of seven died when a mobile goalpost, seemingly unpegged, fell on his head during an organised sports coaching session in West Yorkshire.

To Brenda Smith, of Witham, whose 11-year-old son Jonathan died from a ruptured heart in 1991 after mobile goal posts toppled on him, it is yet another needless tragedy.

She has campaigned ever since the devastating tragedy of Jonathan's death for mobile goalposts to be secured.

Esther Rantzen gave her support to the campaign some years ago when she featured the problem on her then That's Life TV programme. She also came to Witham and met Brenda and her husband.

Despite this, Brenda says, since Jonathan's death there has been, to her knowledge, on average one death a year in this country alone involving unpegged mobile goalposts. Jonathan died eight years ago.

So far the Football Association has issued only 'guidelines' to clubs about mobile goalposts.

Brenda says it is not enough. She is determined, despite the anguish each death brings back to her, to fight on until legislation is brought in making it compulsory for mobile goalposts to be secured in the ground.

She says she cannot give up the fight because each child's death could have been prevented.

DANGERS

It seems to me that Brenda has done everything in her power to highlight the dangers.

We now have a new sports minister, Kate Hoey. I am delighted our MP Alan Hurst has taken up the fight on Brenda and her family's behalf.

Let us see some action on this before another year is out. The legislation required cannot be that complicated.

A Football Goalpost Killed My Son

GAZETTE GOALPOST CAMPAIGN

STOP THESE NEEDLESS DEATHS

Nine years on and Brenda's safety crusade is almost there

● Valuable support – sports minister Kate Hoey reads about the Gazette Goalpost Campaign with Brenda Smith and MP Alan Hurst. *Picture: CLARE BANKS (5802-6)*

VICTORY is in sight for the Gazette's Goalpost campaign.

by MATT PLUMMER

Sports minister Kate Hoey has promised to contact every local authority and education body in Britain about the dangers posed by mobile goalposts.

And she has also pledged to voice her concerns when she meets with Football Association officials next month.

The breakthrough – an important victory for the Gazette's goalpost campaign – followed an eagerly-awaited meeting between Miss Hoey, Essex mum Brenda Smith, whose son Jonathan died when unsecured goalposts collapsed on him in 1991, and Braintree MP Alan Hurst.

Mrs Smith, of Tees Close, Witham, described the experience as "tremendously reassuring".

She said: "Miss Hoey admitted she had been unaware of the extent of the problem and because of that she was very interested in the Gazette campaign.

"She was down to earth, sympathetic and had plenty of interesting points to make.

"To receive encouragement from someone with that kind of profile and authority is amazing. This is the most positive I have felt in nine years of campaigning."

Speaking after the meeting, Miss Hoey told the Gazette she had learnt a great deal from speaking to Mrs Smith.

"I feel the FA could have done more to raise awareness of the dangers of goalposts and I will be raising the matter with them soon," she added.

"We also discussed the possibility of pushing for legislation, although that is obviously a longer term solution."

MP Alan Hurst, who arranged the meeting, said: "We looked at a whole range of ways forward, from circulating information about the dangers of mobile goalposts to discussing what legislation would be most effective."

> " To receive encouragement from someone with that kind of profile and authority is amazing. This is the most positive I have felt in nine years of campaigning. "
>
> BRENDA SMITH

TOP WEBSITE BACKS OUR BID

A Football Goalpost Killed My Son

MPs will debate safety issues

by MATT PLUMMER

HE Gazette's successful alpost campaign has eceived a fresh boost th news safety conrns are to be debated Parliament.

3ob Blizzard, Labour P from Lowestoft, Suf-k, is set to address the ouse of Commons no-row as part of an jot rnment debate.

He intends to discuss e hazards posed by obile posts.

The problem was ought to his attention Ron Harrod, chairman one of Britain's leadg manufacturers, who as featured in the

Gazette's campaign last year.

We launched our fight for tough new safety standards on mobile goalposts with the help of Witham mum Brenda Smith, whose son Jonathan died when mobile post collapsed on him.

Our campaign won the backing of Sports Minister Kate Hoey.

She wrote to every LEA in England and Wales warning them of the danger and launched a major

safety investigation.

She also pledged to look into the possibility of safety legislation.

Now Mr Blizzard is backing the fight to make posts even safer.

He said: "Most manufacturers are responsible enough to provide anchoring pegs, but not all of them do.

"Mr Harrod has been pushing for a UK standard and I will be highlighting this during the debate and making reference to the deaths caused by posts falling over."

Brenda Smith described the

development as "fantastic news".

Mrs Smith, of Tees Close, added: "I'm really pleased because this is exactly what we've been waiting for.

"It's so important to keep the pressure up because until legislation is introduced there's always a chance another accident will happen."

Braintree MP Alan Hurst, who helped the Gazette arrange a meeting with Kate Hoey, is set to join in the debate.

He said: "This is an ideal way to keep the issue in the public eye."

The following pages are from a debate the hall at Westminster on January 25th 2000, where MPs and The Sports Minister Kate Hoey discussed goalpost safety, interesting reading.

A Football Goalpost Killed My Son

Mr. Bob Blizzard (Waveney): First, I should say a word about the title of this debate. The aspect of safety that I wish to talk about concerns goalposts. I should make it clear that I am talking not about professional football, but about football played locally on sports fields and recreation grounds, in or out of school, by organised clubs or by groups of people informally. It is an unfortunate and tragic fact that at least nine children have been killed in such circumstances in the past 13 years. Some may be surprised that children are being killed by something as inert as a set of goalposts. The most recent incident occurred last summer. A seven-year-old boy in Dewsbury was killed when free-standing goalposts toppled over, causing a fatal blow to his head, after children had been swinging on the crossbar. That case is being pursued by my right hon. Friend the Member for Dewsbury (Mrs. Taylor). That tragedy was made all the more appalling by the fact that a fatal goalpost accident was first recorded as long ago as 1986, when a seven-year-old boy was killed. In 1990 an eight-year-old boy was killed and then a 12-year-old girl, when a ball kicked with some force again caused a frame to topple over. In 1991 an 11-year-old boy was killed at Witham in Essex. I know that my hon. Friend the Member for Braintree (Mr. Hurst), whose constituency contains that town, wishes to say a word about that.

Mr. Alan Hurst (Braintree): My hon. Friend mentioned the tragic death of the son of my constituent, Mrs. Brenda Smith of Witham. Mrs. Smith has campaigned for many years to draw public attention to the continuing deaths and injuries from dangerous goalposts. Indeed, late last year Mrs. Smith and I met my hon. Friend the Minister, and we were encouraged by her positive response. Does my hon. Friend agree that the way forward is a combination of safe equipment and greater public awareness?

Mr. Blizzard: I agree with those points, but other steps can be taken. One important feature of that incident was the fact that the goalposts were not factory made by a reliable manufacturer—a point that I shall develop later.

In 1994 a six-year-old boy was killed on holiday. Again the crossbar, which was a piece of scaffold pole, toppled over. In 1995 a 13-year-old boy was killed and in 1996 a two-year-old girl. Again in 1996, a 10-year-old girl was killed when posts topped over: one set had been leaning against a wall. It is possible that there were a couple more deaths in 1996, but I do not have details of them. Each of those deaths was a tragedy, but collectively they are a disgrace, because they were all preventable.

I should explain my constituency interest in this matter. A firm in Lowestoft in my constituency, Harrod UK, is the country's leading goalpost manufacturer. It has nothing to do with Harrods, the Knightsbridge version. Harrod UK supplies nearly all the premier league clubs, including Manchester United. It supplied goalposts for

A Football Goalpost Killed My Son

Euro 96 and for the new Cardiff stadium, and will probably do so for the new Wembley stadium too.

The chairman of the company, Mr. Ron Harrod, has campaigned on goalpost safety since 1991. He is a recognised technical expert. He represents this country on the CEN--the European Committee for Standardisation--and has done for the past seven years. He took his campaign to the XThat's Life" programme in 1991 and made representations to Iain Sproat, the Minister in the previous Government, but received little response.

If we analyse this sad list of fatal accidents, we find that they almost all involve free-standing, movable goalposts, particularly the smaller 6 ft size used for five, six and seven-aside games. The goalposts topple forward when someone swings on or applies pressure to the crossbar. Almost all are home made or adapted from factory models by well-meaning people, but with disastrous consequences. That is exemplified by the police report into the Dewsbury case and I am grateful to my right hon. Friend the Member for Dewsbury for showing that to me. The goalposts were originally full-sized posts and had concreted into the ground, but they had been taken down and adapted. They were heavy--it took three adults to move them--but they were not anchored and of the 21 strong steel spikes that were supplied originally, only one was left and the remainder had been substituted with 10 camping-type pegs, which were not up to the job.

An expert witmess from the Health and Safety Executive stated that, because of the design, only a small amount of force was required to make the posts fall forward under their own weight. Design is the key and it is important to maximise stability to minimise weight. Harrod UK has developed technical solutions to make the posts safe, particularly with the use of anchors, but also with prominent labels on the equipment and bold instruction leaflets. As a result of the campaigning and committee work of people such as Ron Harrod, a European standard--BSEN 748-- now exists for full-sized goalposts. Guidelines and safety warnings have been issued by various organisations, including the HSE, the British Association of Advisers and Lecturers in Physical Education, the Institute of Sport and Recreation Managers and the National Playing Fields Association. The Football Association, through the county associations, advises referees to check them before use. Indeed, the laws of association football require that frames   "must be anchored securely to the ground". Many games, kickabouts and training sessions all over   the country do not take place under FA rules and the guidelines have not stopped accidents and   deaths. Above all, there is not yet a standard for small, free-standing goal posts.

A Football Goalpost Killed My Son

Vital issues remain outstanding. Although a British standard and FA guidelines will make a valuable contribution, they will not alone solve the problem or stop the deaths. The standard will not cover existing goalposts. A standard in this country is voluntary and a manufacturer does not have to adopt it. Most important, we do not have a law making it illegal to make, sell or use non-standard equipment. The new standard will not overcome the main problem, which is the use of homemade or adapted goalposts. By their nature, the pieces of equipment are not made by recognised manufacturers, most of whom would follow the recommended standard. Will my hon. Friend consider the possibility of legislation, so that when safety is involved only equipment that meets the recognised standard is allowed to be sold and used in this country? Will she consider the position in France, where the standard is incorporated into legislation? I understand that it is now illegal in France to make, distribute or use non-standard goalposts. In Germany, a standard is not incorporated in legislation, but I understand that insurance is invalid if non-standard equipment is used, leaving providers and users open to civil proceedings by the injured party. That concentrates the mind and introduces a safety culture.

The standard may give us a safe product, but how do we ensure that goalposts are used properly and safely? How do we ensure that the anchors, which are the answer to the problem, are utilised routinely? The police inquiry into the Dewsbury incident made an interesting point in its conclusion. It said: "There is some concern amongst staff about the role of the HSE and its relationship to Local Authority Environmentally Health for these issues. It is not clear who has responsibility for enforcement. This needs clarifying so that it is clear who has responsibility for enforcement and any future cases."

The HSE wrote to my constituent, Ron Harrod, in 1996, and made the important point that: "sports equipment does not usually fall into the category of work equipment. This means that the provisions of the Health and Safety at Work, etc. Act 1974 concerning the design and manufacture of equipment will not apply. The HSE therefore has no remit in this respect, and all matters of design of sports and play equipment fall to the Department of National Heritage"·· now the Department of Culture, Media and Sport.

I wrote to the HSE at the end of last year, and was told that only two of those nine incidents occurred in circumstances in which the Health and Safety at Work, etc. Act applied, and in which the HSE was the enforcing authority. In the other cases, which often involved children playing with home-made goalposts during their own free time, there was no legal duty on anyone under the Health and Safety at Work, etc. Act. The activities of voluntary football clubs or of children playing on their own would not be covered by the Health and Safety at Work, etc. Act.

A Football Goalpost Killed My Son

My hon. Friend the Member for Braintree came to see me last October with Mrs. Brenda Smith, the mother of Jonathan Smith, who was tragically killed in 1991. I pay tribute to her work over the years in bringing the issue to the attention of those in authority and to everyone in the sport. I gained much valuable information from her and I was struck by her determination to raise awareness of the issue.

I regard it as a priority to make progress on minimum standards for mobile goalposts. Mobile goals designed for use in five-a-side are different from permanent, full-sized goals, which are secured to concrete or other mountings. Permanent goalposts are subject to the British standard BSEN 748, which was introduced in 1996. Mobile goals serve a different purpose, often enabling children to play competitive matches on appropriately sized pitches. They are designed to be dismantled and stored easily, particularly at the end of the match or training session when there is often little room for storage.

A range of mobile goals manufactured by reputable firms in a variety of sizes and specifications has been available to clubs for many years. They are either lightweight constructions of plastic or aluminium or are made of heavier steel pipes, which are designed to be securely anchored in the ground. If fitted and maintained in accordance with the manufacturer's instructions, this equipment is safe to use. However, many of the goals in children's matches are adapted from full-size goals or are constructed on a do-it-yourself basis--often by well-meaning parents who are anxious to help out their sons' or daughters' clubs. The goal that killed Jack Sherrin was cut down from a full-sized one and it was not secured to the ground. The collapse of home-made equipment contructed from scaffolding poles led to the deaths of Jonathan Smith in 1991 and David O'Neill in 1994. I am sure that those goals were built with the best of intentions, but there is no place for dangerously unsafe equipment in sport and there is a clear need for an effective safety standard.

The variety of mobile goals in use makes it difficult to impose standards, which are the responsibility of individual clubs rather than of local government or the football authority. Local authorities are responsible for the design and maintenance of their own facilities, including goalposts and other sports equipment. The Health and Safety at Work Act 1974, as my hon. Friend the Member for Waveney said, requires those who control football pitches used by others to take reasonable measures to ensure the safety of the equipment that they provide. However, the Act does not apply to equipment provided by the users themselves. Most mobile goals owned and used by adult and children's amateur football clubs throughout the country are the responsibility of the clubs themselves, even when club matches are played on local authority pitches.

A Football Goalpost Killed My Son

Raising awareness of this issue with the people who run junior teams is vital. Many demands are placed on those who take on the task of coaching junior teams and arranging matches. I was recently contacted by the manager of an under-eights team in Cheshire, who listed the many stressful duties it is necessary to carry out before a competitive match or training session involving children can kick off. Transport has to be organised, subscriptions collected and playing areas checked for sharp and other dangerous or unpleasant objects. It is a demanding routine, which must often be carried out while supervising excited children. However, my correspondent stressed--I am sure that this view is shared by all those who are involved with young players--that safety must be the primary consideration, and that there must be no compromise on the standards of equipment. I hope that, in time, everyone involved in children's sport will demonstrate a similar awareness of safety issues.

As well as ensuring that those running local football clubs are fully aware of the need to make sure that all equipment is in good condition and that it is used correctly, I am also anxious to encourage the setting of a minimum standard. Following my meetings with manufacturers, I was pleased when many of them-- including the firm that is based in the constituency of my hon. Friend the Member for Waveney--attended a meeting with the FA and the British Standards Institution, where much progress was made.

Setting a British standard is a lengthy process involving much research and consultation. As my hon. Friend said, it can take up to two years. While manufacturers of mobile goalposts are working towards that standard, I am glad to say that they have agreed as a matter of urgency to develop, with the BSI, a public available specification. That will be a much quicker process. The institution has agreed in principle that when the publicly available specification is published, it wi be given fast-track consideration with a view to its forming the basis of a full British standard.

Mr. Blizzard : I am encouraged by what my hon. Friend has said about how much activity is being concentrated on trying to deal with the problem. Could not the authorities include in the circulars that they send out a strong recommendation tha every club or organisation checks to see whether goalposts are from a reliable manufacturer or are of the do-it-yourself variety, and couple that with an equally strong recommendation that they cease using the latter type immediately? Dangerous goalposts could still be in use as we sit here now.

A Football Goalpost Killed My Son

Kate Hoey : My hon. Friend is quite right. Even if we get the standard and make things better for the future, dangerous goalposts could still be in use all around the country. I will suggest strongly that it could be put in that light rather than as just a simple piece of information. The FA and the institution are contributing to the costs of the research work and will issue a joint document shortly, covering the design, use and maintenance of existing mobile equipment. I am pleased that the organisations are working together on this, as it is very important. I hope that I have demonstrated that the Government and I as Minister for Sport take this issue very seriously. Sports safety is becoming more of an issue because increasingly in this country people go to legislation if something happens. Sports, particularly at the voluntary level, will find it difficult if they are involved in costly legislation. It is crucial that they act to avoid the terrible tragedies that can happen to families.

I will continue to meet many of the people involved in manufacturing, regulating and using mobile goals, and to talk to my hon. Friends who have taken an interest. I am sorry that I cannot promise instant legislation. I will look to how we might combine the best efforts of everyone to ensure that the safety aspect is balanced by people themselves being responsible for the measures that they take when they are working with children. I am grateful to my hon. Friend for raising the issue today and for helping to promote the awareness that is so necessary to ensure the safety of our children.

A Football Goalpost Killed My Son

Just before the launch took place, I saw an advert for McDonalds on the television that horrified me; it was of a child swinging on goalposts. I immediately rang the FA and McDonalds and got the advert altered.

Mother wins fight

FAST Food giants McDonalds have cut a scene showing a boy playing on a mobile goal frame from their new television advertisement after a horrified Witham mother told them swinging on the frames could kill.

Brenda Smith's son Jonathan died, aged 12 in 1991, when he was crushed under a heavy steel frame which toppled onto him as he swung from the crossbar during a match.

He would have been 21 on Tuesday.

Mrs Smith, of Tees Road, said: "I was very upset when I saw the advert, although I'm not blaming McDonalds because they were not aware of the situation.

"They have been very apologetic and sympathetic and have promised to back our safety campaign."

The advertisement was shown for the first time on Sunday and is set to be repeated until the European Football Championships this summer.

Victoria Hague, McDonalds' regional communications officer, said: "We are very sorry for any distress caused to the family.

"We consulted with the Football Association as soon as the issue was brought to our attention and immediately edited the advert accordingly."

Mrs Smith has been lobbying the Football Association and MPs for controls over the manufacture and use of mobile goalposts since Jonathan died.

She is about to launch a poster campaign showing her son which has the backing of the FA, sports minister Kate Hoey and former England striker Gary Lineker.

Mrs Smith hopes to get the posters distributed to all schools and football clubs before Euro 2000.

JONATHAN SMITH who died nine year ago when a goalpo fell on him.

A Football Goalpost Killed My Son

t on after complaint from mum of goalpost death boy

McDonald's cut advert scene

by MATT PLUMMER

' food giant ald's has pledged part of its latest mmercial after ng a complaint Witham mum.

ad ert – aired for st time on Sunday , to stay on screen is summer's Euro-Championships – a youngster swing- football goalpost.

it in hours of hear- n Brenda Smith – og ther with the is campaigning for a o o' safety laws – the s vowed to ban the

mith, of Tees Close, son, Jonathan, in her, he was hit by ed goalpost equip- uring a match. He

would have celebrated his 21st birthday yesterday.

She said: "I have to say I was quite upset when I saw the advert, although I'm not blaming McDonald's because they weren't aware of the situation.

"Since then they've been very apologetic and sympa- thetic and have promised to support the Gazette's campaign."

Victoria Hague, McDon- ald's regional communica- tions officer, added: "We are very sorry for any distress caused to the family.

"We consulted with the Football Association as soon as the issue was brought to our attention and immedi- ately edited the advert accordingly."

Meanwhile, Mrs Smith will help rubber-stamp the final design of a poster promoting goalpost safety.

The A3 poster – set to fea- ture a photograph of Jonathan – has been spear- headed by the FA and sports minister Kate Hoey.

It also has the backing of safety bodies like the British Standards Institute and will be distributed to all schools and football clubs in England.

Organisers hope the poster will be unveiled before Euro 2000 and aim to get a host of football celebrities involved.

Peter Henderson, the FA's special projects manager, said: "The poster is a compro- mise between essential infor- mation and a design which is lively and interesting enough to make children take notice."

Our campaign has drawn big support

WITHAM mum Brenda Smith helped launch the Gazette's campaign for a shake-up of safety laws after the tragic death of Jack Sheerin last summer.

The seven-year-old died when a steel post toppled over during a football coaching session near his home in Dewsbury, West Yorkshire.

Since then, various organisations and celebrities have backed our campaign, including the Football Association, former England striker Gary Lineker and ex-Arsenal and Scotland goalkeeper Bob Wilson.

The campaign scored another success when Premiership giants Tottenham Hotspur, Arsenal and West Ham supported our fight for new safety standards.

But the real high came in October when Mrs Smith, the Gazette and Braintree MP Alan Hurst travelled to London to meet sports minister Kate Hoey.

She promised to contact every local authority and education body in Britain about the dangers posed by mobile goalposts. She also pledged to voice her concerns to the Football Association.

A quick response

GOOD for McDonald's for responding so positively and quickly over its latest TV commercial, which showed a child swinging on a football goalpost.

It has now scrapped the sequence from the advert.

I was horrified when I saw it and so, obviously, was Brenda Smith, who, with the Evening Gazette, is campaigning for a shake-up of safety laws.

Mrs Smith's son Jonathan died in 1991 when an unsecured mobile goalpost collapsed on him.

McDonald's, when the facts were drawn to its attention, apologised, agreed to support the campaign for more safety and edited the advert right away.

It all goes to show that there are still people who do not understand the dangers that can be involved, which is why the campaign is so vital.

Although I had a quick response about the television advert for McDonalds I decided to do a survey of the FA's leaflets that should have been distributed, I did this with Nicky. The results were not good. Half the schools that we surveyed had no knowledge of the leaflets and also the response from clubs and local authorities we the same. This got me thinking again to who had seen the leaflets, were they just filed away in a drawer.

The problem now was to get the FA to get the launch arranged, I knew that the leaflets had been printed but nothing else seemed to be happening. I had waited years for this break through and yet months from the leaflets being ready nothing had happened. I decided to write to the Queen as Patron of the FA and explain the situation. I was amazed at the reply in a few days and also the response from the FA with a launch date!

A Football Goalpost Killed My Son

HM The Queen
Buckingham Place
London
11th July 2000

Madam

I am writing to you as Patron of the Football Association.
For the last 9 years I have been tirelessly campaigning for goalpost safety. My son, Jonathan, was tragically killed in January 1991 by a goalpost that fell, as it was unsecured, and ruptured his heart.

After the initial grieving period I discovered, although it had been reported as a tragic accident, that other children had died and several had been injured in similar circumstances.

My first experience of the Football association was in August of 1991 when I travelled up to Lancaster Gate from Essex when I was 8 months pregnant. I was supposed to meet with Graham Kelly, Chief Executive at the time, but I did not. I was fobbed off with one of his underlings. It was not a successful meeting and I was very upset by the response. Over the years I have been very hurt by the continual deaths of children and have campaigned each time to bring public awareness about the dangers of mobile goalposts. Last year a 7 year old boy from Dewsbury died and this has really hit me hard as my daughter is the same age. After a few weeks I made contact with the family and we are now united in our fight.

Both families have had separate meetings with the Minister of Sport, Kate Hoey, who with her staff have been extremely supportive in our campaign.

A poster was to be launched this year before the European Cup in a high profile media launch which the Football Association should have organized and promised to support. They have had

A Football Goalpost Killed My Son

100,000 posters printed with safety guidelines on them to be distributed to local authorities and councils to promote the safety of goalposts. This was meant to be in May, then June, and now who knows. Fortunately today I have been interviewed by the BBC as the British Standards Institution have brought out guideline and advertised these as they are unsure of the Football Association's involvement, because every time anyone rings no-one is available and if a message left they do not ring back.

As you can tell I am extremely cross and as Patron I feel you should be aware of their customer service, general attitude and open promises. I must add that I don't hold them responsible but as an organization in football people look to them for guidance which, as Jack Sheerin's mother from Dewsbury would say, if they had listened to my reasoning 9 years ago, her son would be alive today.

The posters that have been printed are probably sitting in a cupboard and will now be forgotten,
Thank you for reading this.

Yours faithfully

Brenda Smith (Mrs)

A Football Goalpost Killed My Son

BUCKINGHAM PALACE

21st July, 2000

Dear Mrs. Smith,

The Queen has asked me to thank you for your further letter concerning the tragic death of your son, Jonathan, in January 1991, as a result of an unsecured goal post falling on him. Her Majesty, who well recalls your previous letter on the subject in 1992, has taken careful note of your criticism of the Football Association in relation to the safety campaign concerning these mobile goalposts.

It is not possible for The Queen to intervene personally in the administration of the hundreds of organisations with which she is connected, but I have been instructed to forward your letter to the headquarters of the Association so that they may consider the points which you raise in it.

Yours sincerely,

MRS. DEBORAH BEAN
Chief Correspondence Officer

Mrs. Brenda Smith

A Football Goalpost Killed My Son

FA criticised by campaigner

by NEIL JONES

A WITHAM safety campaigner who has fought for nine years to highlight the danger of goalposts has criticised the Football Association for not living up to its promises.

Brenda Smith's 11-year-old son Jonathan died in 1991 when an unsecured goalpost fell on top of him.

Following an Evening Gazette campaign run a year ago to help Mrs Smith change the law, the Football Association launched its own goalpost safety campaign in August.

The association promised to deliver more than 100,000 posters and leaflets to every club, league and school in the country outlining the potential dangers of using goalposts without undertaking the necessary checks and precautions.

But this week less than five per cent of the schools in the Braintree and Witham area said they had received the posters.

Mrs Smith said: "They promised to deliver a poster to every school before the new school year started – which hasn't been done.

"Perhaps the schools themselves should get in contact with the FA and make them send them a poster."

Nick Barron, press officer at the FA, said every school in the country would get a poster but it would take some time.

He said: "Every county F. has been given posters whic they are in turn delivering t clubs.

"We are doing are best t get them out to schools at th moment but it is taking som time.

"We are also in the proces of making another print ru of posters."

neil_jones@thisisessex.co.u

The response from the Queen and also the FA were very quick and the launch then went ahead a few weeks later.

Strange how things happen!

Still writing to Sports personalities, to get more support for the campaign. Received a letter from Gary Lineker, also 2 hand written letters from Bob Wilson, which was very touching.

38

A Football Goalpost Killed My Son

Dear Mrs. Smith,

Thank you for your letter of 9 January which has taken a while to reach me.

I was so sorry to hear of the tragic loss of your son, Jonathan, and also the other children who seem to have lost their lives so needlessly. I would be happy to support your campaign for safer mobile goalposts. As the parent of four football-mad boys I feel their safety is absolutely imperative.

Yours sincerely

GARY LINEKER

A Football Goalpost Killed My Son

Letters from Bob Wilson next:

Dear Brenda.

Thankyou for your letter, albeit it
such a sad one. How I feel for you
over Jonathan's death.

Having run Goalkeeping Schools
for some thirteen years one were so
aware of rules and regulations regarding
the anchoring of Goals. I thought these
rules were made law but obviously not.

Anyway. If you want my support
then you can certainly have it. Good
luck with your work.

With best wishes
Yours Sincerely.

Bob Wilson

Dear Brenda,

Thank you for your letter and all the cuttings and information collected so far.

I think the main publicity could be gained during the meeting with Kate Hoey in April. Are you going yourself, and what sort of photo opportunities are there then?

With best wishes
Yours sincerely

Bob Hind Sen.

Football celebrity joins our safety bid

GAZETTE GOALPOST CAMPAIGN

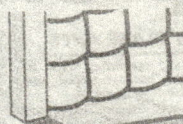

STOP THESE NEEDLESS DEATHS

by MATT PLUMMER

FORMER Arsenal and Scotland goalkeeper Bob Wilson has shown a safe pair of hands – by catching the chance to back the Gazette's successful goalpost campaign.

The ITV football anchorman was responding to a letter written by Witham mum Brenda Smith, whose son Jonathan died when a set of posts collapsed on him in 1991.

Mrs Smith, of Tees Close, helped launch our drive for a shake-up of safety laws after the death of seven-year-old Jack Sheerin, from Lancashire, in similar circumstances.

Mr Wilson wrote: "How I feel for you over Jonathan's death.

"Having run goalkeeping schools for some 13 years we are so aware of rules and regulations regarding the anchoring of goals.

"Anyway, if you want my support then you can certainly have it. Good luck with your work."

Mrs Smith described the reply as "exceptionally genuine."

She added: "I was delighted to receive such a lovely letter and now I'm going to send the Gazette's goalpost articles to Mr Wilson so he's got all the background information at hand.

"It's so important to get the backing of celebrities because children take notice of them and, in many cases, idolise them."

Others who have backed our campaign include former England striker Gary Lineker, Spurs manager George Graham, Arsenal boss Arsene Wenger and West Ham's Harry Redknapp.

Mrs Smith travelled with the Gazette and Braintree MP Alan Hurst to meet sports minister Kate Hoey.

She promised to contact every local authority and education body in Britain about the dangers posed by mobile goalposts, and she pledged to voice her concerns to the

● Joining up – TV soccer expert Bob Wilson.

Football Association.

● Manchester United fan Jack Sheerin was killed by rickety goalposts during a coaching session near his home in Dewsbury, West Yorkshire, last summer.

Now his mum, Susan, has been granted a meeting with Miss Hoey on April 12 to further discuss new safety measures.

42

A Football Goalpost Killed My Son

GAZETTE
GOALPOST
CAMPAIGN

STOP THESE
NEEDLESS
DEATHS

Gary backs campaign

● Gary Lineker

by MATT PLUMMER

FORMER England striker Gary Lineker has backed the Gazette's successful goalpost campaign.

The Match of the Day host responded to a letter written by Witham mum Brenda Smith, whose son Jonathan died when a set of goalposts collapsed on him in 1991.

Mrs Smith, of Tees Close, helped us launch our drive last year for new safety measures after the death of seven-year-old Jack Sherrin in similar circumstances.

The former England frontman wrote: "I was so sorry to hear of the tragic loss of your son, Jonathan, and also the other children who seem to have lost their lives so needlessly.

"I would be happy to support your campaign for safer mobile goalposts. As a parent of four football-mad boys I feel their safety is absolutely imperative."

Mrs Smith, of Tees Close, said: "Gary was always a favourite of mine when he was playing for England so I'm delighted he is going to put his name to our campaign.

"Things have gone a bit quiet lately so this is a real boost. Gary could have ignored my letter – he probably gets sackfuls of mail – but this proves he cares."

Others who have backed our campaign include Spurs manager George Graham, Arsenal boss Arsene Wenger and West Ham's Harry Redknapp.

Mrs Smith travelled with the Gazette and Braintree MP Alan Hurst to meet sports minister Kate Hoey.

She promised to contact every local authority and education body in Britain about the dangers posed by mobile goalposts, and she pledged to voice her concerns to the Football Association.

43

A Football Goalpost Killed My Son

Our Ref: AC-0127

4 August 2000

THE FOOTBALL
ASSOCIATION

PATRON
Her Majesty The Queen
PRESIDENT
H.R.H. The Duke of Kent

16 Lancaster Gate
London W2 3LW

Direct Tel: 020 7314 523
Direct Fax: 020 7314 531

Dear Mrs. Smith,

I took over as Chief Executive of The Football Association earlier this year and wanted to write you to introduce myself and ask if you could spare some time to meet with me in the near future.

I was recently taken through the sad events surrounding your son Jonathan and indeed the details of your relationship with The F.A. since then and felt it would be a good idea to meet.

I'm sure you are aware by now that The F.A. plans to launch a safety campaign next week in partnership with government but I'm equally sure that there may be many other issues you would wish to discuss.

As I don't have a telephone number for you I wonder if I could ask you to call me on 020 7314 5236 to fix up a time which would be suitable for you.

I hope we will be able to meet soon and in the meantime please don't hesitate to call if I can help in any way.

Yours sincerely,

ADAM CROZIER
Chief Executive

A Football Goalpost Killed My Son

The campaign continued with as much strength as we could. Susan and I both had long discussions with the new Chief Executive of the Football Association Adam Crozier. All this lead to the launch of the leaflet/ poster that Susan and I had both wanted. It would also give Susan and me the opportunity to meet face to face.

The website for the goalpost safety campaign can be found: www.TheFA.com

The leaflet features Jonathan and Jack and the goalpost safety message:

Check it!
Secure it!
Test it!
Respect it!

Unfortunately Susan couldn't make the leaflet/poster launch as it was held at Watford Football ground which was nearer to me than her. My good friend Nicky came with me on the day. Nicky has been such a great support to me through all my campaigning, always making herself available to come with me to meetings.

A Football Goalpost Killed My Son

Soccer safety posters

ec db 150800 22 01 26

A WITHAM mother who has been fighting for improved safety standards in portable soccer goalposts since her son died in a tragic accident has launched a national poster and leaflet campaign.

A total of 100,000 posters have been printed by the Football Association for schools, football clubs and councils, thanks to the efforts of Mrs Brenda Smith of Tees Close.

The promotion, which advises on safety in erecting and fixing portable goalposts, was launched at Watford Football Club last week by chief executive of the FA, Adam Crozier, former England goalkeeper, Ray Clemence and Braintree MP, Alan Hurst who has supported the campaign.

Mrs Smith's son Jonathan died in 1991 from a ruptured heart after a portable goalpost fell onto him.

TIRELESS CAMPAIGN: Brenda Smith with the new FA goalpost safety poster.

A Football Goalpost Killed My Son

Nine years on, Brenda won't stop fighting

LAST week the Football Association launched a poster campaign to highlight the dangers of unsecured goalposts.

It follows nine years of dedicated and courageous campaigning by Witham mother Brenda Smith, whose son Jonathan died at the age of 11 when an unsecured goalpost fell on him.

Since Jonathan's death in 1991, nine more children have died in similar circumstances.

Each of those deaths has caused Brenda, tormented by her own grief over Jonathan, more anguish.

Her fight to get legislation over the pegging of mobile goalposts goes on.

But that so much has been achieved so far – last month the British Standards Institute unveiled new guidelines for goalpost safety and now the FA has thrown its considerable weight and influence behind the campaign – is due to Brenda's steadfast determination.

It has not been easy to get things moving.

Nine years is a long time to wait.

Many people would have given up long ago and said: "I've done my bit; let someone else take up the fight."

Brenda has never done that, even at the worst times.

She also has a disabled child, Laura, to care for.

A year ago, following the death of seven-year-old Jack Sheerin, Brenda's campaign intensified and the Evening Gazette launched its own goalpost campaign to support her.

After the launch of the Football Association's poster campaign Brenda told me: "I will never give up until we have actual legislation."

I know she won't.

She will fight on through all the disappointments and setbacks until she feels children can play football safely.

I remember when Jonathan died and someone, with the best intentions, tried to keep a group of his childhood friends from coming to see Brenda and "bothering" her at that time.

And I remember Brenda's response. "Let them come in. I want to see them."

She loves children and cares deeply about their safety.

She has lost her own son. It need not have happened and nor need the other nine deaths since that terrible day.

Football Association chief executive Adam Crozier says: "Everyone involved with playing and organising football must play their part to ensure that the tragic accidents that have so disfigured the game in the past never happen again."

Sports minister Kate Hoey, who met Brenda earlier this year, says children playing sport must be protected and there "must be no compromise on the standard of equipment."

The Queen is patron of the Football Association and Brenda wrote to her earlier this year, anxious to get the poster campaign under way.

Now it is.

Braintree MP Alan Hurst, who was at the launch of the campaign, has, says Brenda, given enormous support.

If anyone deserves it, she does.

● TUESDAY: ST JOHN'S, HIGH WOODS and GREENSTEAD **● WEDNESDAY:** TIPTREE and MERSEA **● THURSDAY:** BRIGHTLINGSEA and WIVENHOE **● FRIDAY:** OLD HEATH & NEW TOWN and STANWAY

Together with Nicky we did a survey on how the leaflets/posters had been distributed and the results were not good, hence following letters.

A Football Goalpost Killed My Son

31/08/2000

Dear Adam,

Yesterday I spoke to Alex Stone in your customer liaison department so ask about the publicity of the poster. The only press reports that I had seen were the ones that I myself had been involved with. I must say that I was somewhat disappointed at the media response. Over the last week I have been doing my own research as to the receipt of the leaflets / posters, which I felt necessary because of my past history with the F.A. It had been stated in the letter that I received on the 4th August 2000 that, I quote, 'As well as ensuring that we brief national and regional press, we will then distribute briefing notes and photos to bodies such as the Local Government Associations, The National Playing Fields Association and Physical Education Association.' The National Playing Fields Association and the Local Government Association have not received any information to date, one out of three of the local councils in my area have received a poster the other two were unsure. Also last week I had a telephone conversation with a local leisure centre asking me to go and give them a risk assessment of the mobile goals inuse. They had seen my name in the local newspaper and wanted my advice. I explained that I had a great deal of knowledge but for health and safety reasons I could not advise them.

Adam want I really want to say is that over the last 9 years the relationship that I have had with the F.A. has been non-existent, I feel now that you understand the importance of what I am trying to achieve and although you may say that it is early days we still need to do so much more, which I cannot do on my own. The chap that I spoke to at the local council had the poster up on his wall in his office, which he shares with 4 other people; message will only therefore reach those people he sits with.

The posters need to be on bill boards throughout the country and as McDonalds had an interest when the advert of a child swinging on a goalpost was altered, because I telephoned them and asked them after explaining the situation. They have so many outlets and also advertise at large football grounds, I feel sure that they would be willing to display posters promoting the safety of mobile goalposts.

I will arrange to come and have a meeting with you when my daughter is settled back at school probably towards the end of September.

A Football Goalpost Killed My Son

Thank you for taking the time to read this, and really as I am only a member of the public which through unfortunate circumstance's in losing my son, I don't feel that is my job to check up on a large organisation like yours.

Yours sincerely

Brenda Smith

A Football Goalpost Killed My Son

Department for Culture, Media and Sport
Minister for Sport
Kate Hoey MP

2-4 Cockspur Street
London SW1Y 5DH
www.culture.gov.uk

Tel 020-7211 6246
Fax 020-7211 6249

C00/13122/04636/DC

8 September 2000

Dear Brenda

Thank you for your letter of 31 August.

I should firstly say that I was sorry that I was not able to attend the launch of the FA's mobile goalpost safety poster on 10 August at Vicarage Road. As you know, I take this issue very seriously, and I would like to have had the opportunity to support the campaign in person. I'm afraid the FA fixed the date without first checking when I was on holiday.

I understand that the launch went very well, and that you had a useful initial discussion with Adam Crozier. However, I was disturbed to learn of your subsequent findings about the distribution of the posters. I agree that the FA must ensure that the posters are forwarded to all clubs, schools and sports centres where mobile equipment is used, and that they must be prominently displayed in a position where they will be seen by players, coaches and teachers.

My officials have spoken to the FA this week. It seems that the distribution of the 100,000 posters is still continuing, but that every school in the country should shortly receive one along with clubs (through the County FA system), local authorities and other bodies. That is encouraging, but DCMS will also check on the position through our own contacts over the next few weeks. I very much hope that the FA's distribution of this vital information will have improved by the end of that period.

I am sure that you will bring these matters to Adam Crozier's attention when you meet him for a longer discussion.

INVESTOR IN PEOPLE

A Football Goalpost Killed My Son

More generally, my Department is continuing its research on legislation abroad, and we hope to receive full details of the operation of French legislation shortly. That information should put us in a position to fully consider the case for legislation in the UK, and (with the FA) to investigate the possibility of a large scale testing and remedial programme for goalposts through the Football Foundation. As you say in your letter, this work will take time, but I very much hope that we can advise you of some progress shortly.

Best wishes.

Yours sincerely

Kate

KATE HOEY
Minister for Sport

Perhaps the Premier League could be asked to try to get their clubs programmes to carry the advert/poster.

Cash hope in goalposts safety plea

A WITHAM mother's campaign for safer soccer goalposts after the tragic death of her son looks set to be boosted by millions of pounds.

Mrs Brenda Smith, of Tees Close, has been fighting for better safety since her 11-year-old son Jonathan died in 1991 when a goalpost fell on him.

Now a campaign, agreed by the Football Premier League the Football Association and Sport England, to distribute posters and leaflets to clubs, schools and organisations across the country is set to get a higher profile.

Organisers are hopeful that the newly-formed Football Foundation may help fund a multi-million pound scheme to set up assessors to check on every goalpost, both portable and fixed throughout the coun-

By Rod Andrews

try, and to help pay for repairs to bring them up to standard.

Mr Sean Coster, a spokesman for the Department of Culture, Media and Sport in London explained this week: "The scheme is in the early stages yet, but we are very hopeful of a successful outcome.

"There is still research to be carried out into safety elements, discussions about who will carry out the testing and oversee it, and of course funding.

"To put the issue into perspective, there are estimated to be over 220,000 sets of goalposts in England alone which would need inspecting, and the detail associated with any repair work.

"We have to put a formal proposition to the Football Foundation, but I would hope to

see some real progress by the end of this football season."

Brenda Smith said: "I am delighted at the way this all seems to be moving forward. I have been asked if I will be involved and will be happy to agree.

"During the last week I had a further meeting with Mr Adam Crosier of the Football Association and he is behind the whole scheme.

"Leaflets and posters were given out at the recent England Under-23 game and during the England/Germany match.

"I had asked to see Mr Crozier again because I was worried that not enough of the leaflets were being distributed, but he has reassured me that things are under way and these new developments are a real breakthrough."

A Football Goalpost Killed My Son

Great news from the Department of Cultural Media and Sport: A newly formed Football Foundation may help to fund a million pound scheme to set up assessors to check on every goalpost, both portable and fixed throughout the country, and help to pay for repairs to bring them up to standard. I am now beginning to feel that all my time and campaigning will be a great success.

Pages that follow included letters and press cuttings relevant to the campaign.

A Football Goalpost Killed My Son

Our Ref: AC-0247

13 November 2000

THE FOOTBALL
ASSOCIATION

PATRON
Her Majesty The Queen
PRESIDENT
H.R.H. The Duke of York CBO ADC

25 Soho Square
London W1D 4FA
www.the-fa.org

Direct Tel: 020 7745 4577
Direct Fax: 020 7745 5577

Dear Brenda,

Following our meeting I promised to write to you and confirm a date by which we felt all the leaflets would be distributed.

Having checked with the team, the situation is as follows:

- All county F.A.'s have been sent leaflets to distribute to the club in their area.
- All counties, with the exception of Cumberland/Durham and Oxford University, have confirmed that their clubs have received the mail out.
- We will chase the three counties this week to ensure they are distributed.
- By the end of November all schools will have received the leaflets.

Brenda, I think the next urgent stage is for us to write to all clubs/schools/counties to give recommendations on how/where the leaflets and posters should be displayed. Also, how the position should be monitored in terms of how the rules are followed.

I will get Mark Sudbury here at The F.A. to construct a letter, which we will send to you for your comments, before it goes out.

I hope this answers your question about the current state of play but please call me if you have any questions at all.

Kindest regards,

A. Evans.

p.p. ADAM CROZIER
Chief Executive

cc   Mark Sudbury

A Football Goalpost Killed My Son

Mr Adam Crozier (Personal)
The Football Association Limited
25 Soho Square
LONDON
W1D 4FA

2 February 2001

Dear Adam

I am writing to remind you that I am still waiting to hear re the content of your letter of 13 November 2000.

I spoke to your Secretary on 5 January 2001 to express my concern re lack of feedback from you.

Adam, I am extremely disappointed in the lack of commitment from your organisation. I had really good vibes after our October meeting and felt that you were behind my campaign, I have yet to see any indication that the original leaflets have been distributed anywhere. Both myself and my local paper have surveyed local clubs and schools and found that very few have received anything. To hear about a fact sheet that the FA have supported re Free Standing Goal Frames third hand has also upset me, especially when the press telephoned and wanted me to comment on this.

I need to know whether all clubs/schools/counties have been given recommendations on how/where the leaflets and posters should be displayed and also how the position will be monitored in terms of these rules being followed.

Your letter of 13 November invited me to call if I had any questions at all. I have called on a number of occasions, but have not received a call back. One of the last things you said to me at our meeting in October was "If we are doing anything wrong – let us know." I said I would, but it seems my approaches are being ignored.

Yours sincerely

Brenda Smith

cc: Kate Hoey MP
    Sean Coster
    Essex County Newspapers

A Football Goalpost Killed My Son

University of Leicester in mid-January 2001 after certain members of their Administration became aware of the work done by one of their own employees.

Can I also take this opportunity to give you the latest information on the distribution of leaflets, following on from our previous update late last year.

We have recently received a request from a national youth organisation based in London who want to distribute 3,000 copies of the leaflet in their next mailing, which will be in either March or April.

A further 10,000 leaflets are also due to be distributed over the coming months to Football clubs across the country who are applying for The F.A. Charter Standard for clubs. The Charter Standard when awarded will enable children and parents alike to recognise that a Charter Standard club is one that adheres to the F.A. Code of Good Practice, which includes awareness of, and implementation of the guidelines in the Goalpost Safety leaflet.

For the future, The F.A. will be launching a Football Roadshow later on this year, which will tour around the country at footballing venues in the days prior to important matches. These roadshows will communicate to the local public exactly what type of work The F.A. are involved in, and it is our intention to make goalpost safety one of the many issues that we wish to continue to inform adults and children alike about.

I hope that the information above will confirm that The F.A. is as firmly committed to this issue as we have ever been, and should you come across people who have not received a copy of the goalpost safety leaflet, we would be happy to send them as many copies as they require. To make their request, they should contact Alex Stone directly on 0207 7454704.

We will endeavour to keep you better updated on progress, and please do contact us with any queries or concerns.

Kind Regards,

Yours sincerely

Mark Sudbury
Head of Customer Relations

cc Minister for Sport
   Sean Coster, DCMS

A Football Goalpost Killed My Son

Our Ref: GPS-MAY01

17th May 2001

THE FOOTBALL ASSOCIATION

PATRON
Her Majesty The Queen
PRESIDENT
HRH The Duke of York, CVO, ADC

25 Soho Square
London W1D 4FA
www.the-fa.org

Dear Brenda,

Following the work around the Easter holidays, I thought I would give you a quick update.

Enclosed you will find the latest copy of the mini-soccer goalpost catalogue, which contains both the guidelines and the poster, and a photocopied article which appeared in last weekend's F.A. Cup Final programme, of which 100,000 copies were printed and purchased.

The most exciting development since Easter, and arguably for a long time has emerged this week, after a meeting between Mike Appleby, F.A. National Facilities Manager, and a company called CST (Centre for Sports Technology) in Greenwich.

CST have been working on developing a 'test' for goalposts, which is based on testing the crossbar strength, and the stability of the goalposts (whether they will topple over if weight is put on them), to conform to the European CEN standards.

Mike was initially impressed with the prototype, and is also aware that there are two companies in Bradford and Sheffield who have been also developing similar tests, and he also intends to find out more about.

At this stage we are looking at inviting these three companies, and any others to submit a tender to us, with the purpose of carrying out a series of random tests on a minimum of 200 sets of goalposts, both fixed and free standing.

Choosing a company to work in partnership with us will be relatively straightforward. The second part of this process will be to determine who will be responsible for the funding of goalposts which fail the proposed 'test'. At present, it is estimated that 80% of all football facilities are operated by local authorities, and the issue of funding will no doubt be something that The F.A. , Football Foundation and Government will need to discuss further down the line.

If you have any questions from this, obviously feel free to give me a call. However, the intended timescale for choosing a testing partner is envisaged to be by mid-July, and if there are any developments on this, I will inform you immediately.

Regards,

Alex Stone

A Football Goalpost Killed My Son

Department for Culture, Media and Sport
The Rt Hon Richard Caborn MP
Minister for Sport

2-4 Cockspur Street
London SW1Y 5DH
www.culture.gov.uk

Tel 020-7211 6247
Fax 020-7211 6249

C01/08986/03200/DC

Alan Hurst MP
House of Commons
LONDON
SW1A 0AA

15 July 2001

Dear Alan

Thank you for your letter of 5 July about your constituent, Mrs Brenda Smith of 12 Tees Close, Witham, Essex CM8 1LG.

I understand that Brenda met Kate Hoey late in 1999, and that Kate later met Tony and Susan Sheerin, who also lost their son in a tragic accident involving mobile goalposts. Since those meetings, DCMS has worked with the FA, the Health & Safety Executive and other organisations in publicising the dangers of home-made and poorly-maintained goalposts, and towards putting measures in place to ensure that new and existing goals are safe in use.

As you say, the FA published new guidelines as part of a major publicity campaign last summer, and since then my Department has been working with the Association and the Football Foundation on a possible testing and repair scheme for existing equipment.

As you know, Adam Crozier met Mrs Smith to discuss these matters last October. I intend to raise the issue when I meet him early in September, and I will let you know the outcome of that discussion.

Yours sincerely

Richard

THE RT HON RICHARD CABORN MP
Minister for Sport

A Football Goalpost Killed My Son

Ms Kate Hoey MP
House of Commons
LONDON SW1A OAA

30 November 2001

Dear Kate

FOOTBALL GOALPOSTS

I am contacting you as I hope you may be able to continue supporting me in my long, ongoing goalpost safety campaign. After 10 years of hard campaigning there is still no safety legislation in place.

The Football Association was supposed to be carrying out a testing programme on goalposts, which should have been up and running in September. Because of legal arguments they have yet to implement this. I spoke to them yesterday, 29 November, and was told a meeting about this will be taking place on 13 December 2001 .

Unfortunately on Wednesday yet another child was badly bruised when a tubular metal goalpost fell on him. He was on his school playing field and fortunately his teacher was with him. This, to be honest, sickens me a great deal. Especially as the accident happened in Brightlingsea, Essex, only about 20 miles from where I live, which is an area where there has been much publicity in local papers and on both television and local radio, over a long period of time. Still the message is not getting through to schools and sports clubs. I have spoken to Sean Coster of DCMS and Alan Hurst's office and Alan's secretary is going to contact the MP for the area in which the last accident occurred.

I obviously want to continue with my campaign and need as much backing as possible to enable me to have a meeting with the new Sports Minister.

Yours sincerely,

Brenda Smith

A Football Goalpost Killed My Son

by CHRIS McWILLIAMS

THOUSANDS of leaflets promoting a Witham mum's campaign to make football goalposts safer have been handed out at England soccer games.

The campaign is being spearheaded by Brenda Smith, of Tees Close, whose 11-year-old son Jonathan died in 1991 after a goalpost fell on him.

About 15,000 leaflets, produced by the Football Association, were distributed at the under-21 game in Derby on Friday and the England-Germany showdown at Wembley on Saturday.

It is hoped the leaflet drop will raise the nationwide profile of the campaign which is backed by the Times' sister paper the Evening Gazette.

Mrs Smith met FA chief executive Adam Crozier last week to discuss the ongoing campaign and was "gobsmacked" by how it has gathered momentum.

She said: "We had an extremely positive meeting. They are quite committed.

"We're still looking towards legislation. People say we're not going to achieve it but I will achieve it."

Leaflets should eventually be sent to thousands of schools and junior football clubs around the country, Mrs Smith added.

The goalpost campaign could be boosted further with news the Football Foundation – set up by the Government in July to support grass roots soccer – may put millions of pounds towards a goalpost testing scheme across England.

Sean Coster, from the Department of Culture, Media and Sport, said: "We would like to support this major national scheme of restoring and repairing goalposts to make sure these tragedies don't happen again."

● Brenda Smith, who was promised a further update letter from the FA this week, said she was not expecting it quite yet.

She suspected the chief executive Adam Crozier might have other things on his mind – like finding a new England manager after Kevin Keegan's dramatic walk-out on Saturday.

"I won't press the issue this week. I will give him grace because of what has happened," she said.

LETTER OF THE WEEK

£50 Each week for the tender

FOOTBALL GOALPOSTS

How reassuring it was to read about your campaign for football safety in your feature *'Nine kids killed playing football'* in Issue 30.

It's a scandal that's happening all over the world — our dear, seven-year-old grandson, Neil Montgomery, was killed by a free-standing goalpost in Australia in 1987. My daughter has spent many years campaigning for their abolition, and to see others campaigning too means that, hopefully, we will see an end to this danger.

K Montgomery, Birmingham

Recently Bella magazine had printed an article about goalpost safety and a few weeks later this appeared on the letters page of the magazine.

A Football Goalpost Killed My Son

Goalposts still causing worry

23-4-02

All the news from Witham with EVE SWEETING

FIRST FOR WITHAM NEWS

R 11 long years, she ...elessly campaigned to ...t safer goalposts ...oss the country and ...now she hoped she ...uld be able to relax a ...le, in the knowledge ...at the message had got ...me and no more lives ...uld be lost.

...ut Witham mother ...enda Smith is still ...shocked by constant reminders of the tragic death of her 11-year-old son Jonathan, who was killed in 1991 when a set of insecure goalposts collapsed on top of him.

Last week, she was horrified to see, just 100 yards from the cemetery where Jonathan is buried, vandalised goalposts on the recreation ground off Forest Road.

Brenda says the goalposts should be more securely fixed together and concreted into the ground if they are permanently left out.

Braintree Council says it doesn't believe concreting the posts into the ground is possible because if they were broken "we couldn't replace them".

The council adds: "It takes a three-man crew to move them so what can we do to prevent people who are determined to move them I don't know."

I walked around the playing fields off Spa Road and looked at the goalposts there. They are all very rusty.

How often are they checked?

Again, the council has said: "We welcome calls from the public, it's the only way we can monitor things efficiently."

Until Jonathan's death, and the subsequent tragic deaths from similar incidents following it, I had never given goalposts any thought. They were just there so that children could play football.

Now, looking up at the rusting goalposts in the Spa Road playing fields, I know they are not just playthings - they are potential death traps.

The permanent ones should be checked, maintained and checked again because sadly, vandals will always be with us.

As for the mobile goalposts, by the end of the year people should be more educated in how to assemble them, as it will be necessary to have an operator's licence to use them.

After all she has been through, Brenda did not expect to see vandalised goalposts on her own doorstep. She has fought bravely and at times very much on her own, to save other families from the anguish hers has suffered from Jonathan's death. She deserves to be able to move on in her life.

61

A Football Goalpost Killed My Son

C03/05241/02884/pa

Mark Palios
Chief Executive
The Football Association
25 Soho Square
London
W1D 4FA

5 July 2003

Dear Mark

It was good to meet you last week. Congratulations again on your appointment and I look forward to working closely with you and the FA in the future.

I wanted to take this early opportunity to bring to your attention the issue of goalpost safety which the FA have been working on, over the last three years, following the tragic death of a number of children. While I understand that it will not be your first priority as new Chief Executive, I thought it was valuable to emphasise how important this issue is. Your officials will be able to brief you about the details.

I believe that we have a corporate responsibility to all levels of football on a number of related issues, such as goalpost safety. I am keen that we continue to increase awareness, to ensure that all goalposts are safe, and the Goalpost Safety Working Group keep working towards a full British Standard for new goals. I am delighted that goalpost safety was included in the grass roots development strategy announced by the FA earlier this year.

I would be happy to discuss this further with you at some point in the future.

I am copying this letter to Alan Hurst MP and Brenda Smith.

Yours sincerely

Richard C.

RT HON RICHARD CABORN MP
Minister for Sport

A Football Goalpost Killed My Son

16 July 2003

Dear Brenda

Further to my letter to you of 16 June 2003, please find enclosed a copy of the reply I have now received from the new Sports Minister.

I am pleased that the Minister has written to the new Chief Executive of the FA to bring the issue of goal post safety to his attention. I understand that a copy of his letter has also been sent to you direct.

It would seem from the publicity that we have both now been able to read, that the DCMS and the FA are taking the matter seriously. As you can see from the Minister's reply, progress is being made to establishing a full British Standard for goalpost. This, together with increased awareness of the safety issues surrounding goalposts and their proper use, should help make the game safer.

The Minister has promised to keep you updated with further progress. However, if I can be of further assistance please do not hesitate to let me know.

Best wishes,

Yours sincerely

Alan Hurst

A Football Goalpost Killed My Son

Department for Culture, Media and Sport
Rt Hon Richard Caborn MP
Minister for Sport

2-4 Cockspur Street
London SW1Y 5DH
www.culture.gov.uk

Tel   020 7211 6247
Fax   020 7211 6249
richard.caborn @
culture.gsi.gov.uk

C03/05241/02868/pa

Alan Hurst MP
House of Commons
London
SW1A 0AA

9 July 2003

Dear Alan

Thank you for your letter of 16 June about the goal post safety campaign.

Unfortunately, due to my extremely busy diary at present I will not be able to meet with you in the near future. However, I hope that you will find the update below useful. While I am sure that staff at the FA will make their new Chief Executive, Mark Palios, aware of the issues surrounding goal post safety at an early stage, I will also write to him telling him how important this issue is and that this work must be continued.

As you may know, a revised leaflet about goalpost safely was reissued in February 2003 to every amateur club and school in England, I enclose a full distribution list. As well as the FA's guidance note, the National Playing Field Association (NPFA) has continued to distribute detailed guidance on the design and use of both permanent and mobile goalposts. The Institute of Sport and Recreation Management has also produced a detailed note. I was also pleased that the Winter Issue of The National Game, a newsletter for clubs and coaches produced by the FA, featured a prominent article about goalpost safely, which I enclose. I believe that through publicity like this, awareness will continue to improve.

The Goalpost Safety Working Group, which is chaired by Steve Williams, has now met four times since the testing report was issued. Sean Coster from Sports Division here attended three of the meetings and there has been significant progress. The Group is working towards a full British Standard for new goals and to augment the voluntary manufacturers' standard, which you will recall was announced in May 2000. It is also working up detailed technical guidance on the use and testing of goals and I hope this paper will be agreed in the near future.

A Football Goalpost Killed My Son

Goalpost safety has also been prominent in the grass roots development strategy announced by the FA earlier this year. This strategy helps to lock in certain criteria as a condition of funding from the FA.

We are also keeping Brenda Smith fully informed of progress.

Yours sincerely

Richard

RT HON RICHARD CABORN MP
Minister for Sport

A Football Goalpost Killed My Son

Children killed by collapsing goalposts

The Football Association is planning a £1 million initiative to replace unsafe portable goalposts that have been responsible for causing the deaths of dozens of children across the world.

The FA has sent more than a million leaflets to schools and sports clubs warning them that home-made posts should not be used as they, "have been the cause of a huge number of deaths and injuries."

Thirteen children have been killed in recent years and thousands more injured by unsecured goalposts in Britain. More than 20 children have been killed in America by falling posts and crossbars and others have died in Australia, Ireland and Malta.

The British Standards Institution has warned goalpost manufacturers that if their goals do not pass strict test of strength and stability then they will not be able to display its Bsi logo. It is hoped that the threat, backed by the FA and the Department of Culture, Media and Sport, will lead to companies improving their equipment.

Brenda Smith, whose son Jonathan, died aged 11 in 1991 when a goalpost fell on him has been a leading campaigner to ensure that portable posts are made secure. Mrs Smith said: "My constant concern is that the 'man down the street' will continue to make home made goalposts and take no notice of the safety guidelines. "I would urge all parents to check goalposts before their child plays, to make sure they are safe and secure and to prevent any further needless accidents."

Goals are often freestanding and there is no legal obligation to secure them to the ground, so when children swing on them they come crashing down.

A recent FA survey found that 42% of mini soccer goals, 50% of 5-a-side goals and 22% of junior goals failed stability tests. A set of full-sized metal posts blew over during an under 12's game this year at a professional football club.

Legislation will be needed to make sure that unsecured portable posts are banned. Alex Stone from the FA said: " We have put out leaflets but it is for the government to put forward legislation. Some local authorities are continuing to use wooden posts which we have found are the most dangerous."

Click here to link to the official FA guidance regarding goalpost safety.

eNews issue 12

A Football Goalpost Killed My Son

At last The Football Association have come to my way of thinking. As quoted above, 'We have put out leaflets but it is for the government to put forward legislation. Some local authorities are continuing to use wooden posts which we found are the most dangerous.'

This was the best news that I had heard in several years. Sadly I couldn't share it with Susan Sheerin (Jack's Mum) as she had sadly died.

I must carry on the goalpost safety campaign, not only for Jonathan and Jack but now for Susan who showed such commitment.

There are still thousands of unsafe goalposts that still need to be replaced. Now that the Football Foundation have set up funding and can gives grants to clubs to replace unsafe goals there is no excuse.

All information can be found at www.footballfoundation.org.uk

Terrible news from Australia, in June 2003, media in touch with me to get my reaction. What can I say but why has it happened again.

Apparently a 3 year old girl called India Verity died after a portable goalpost fell on her during a soccer gala day. It happened at the Moss Vale Soccer Club gala day on the 28th June 2003, there was nothing holding down the 180kg structure that fell and struck India.

The coroner concluded: the dissemination of information about goalpost safety to local soccer clubs was haphazard, and it would appear that in this case the council, while identifying the concern, did not put into place appropriate action and/or policies to ensure

A Football Goalpost Killed My Son

compliance.

It was then reported that the first identifiable death occurred as far back as 1978, when a thirteen year old died at a school sports day in the town of Ingham, in Far North Queensland.

While official statistics are not catalogued, over the last 26 years in Australia there have been 8 deaths from falling portable soccer goalposts and in 1990 a thirteen year old was rendered a paraplegic.

This doesn't count the other 5 states that don't hold such records.

After the inquest into India, New South Wales issued safety guidelines. www.standards.org.au

Unfortunately soon after I was told about the death in Australia I was informed of one in Ireland. I feel really sick every time I am told about yet other fatalities involving unsafe goalposts. If brings back all the memories of the death of Jonathan.

In Ireland they announced a formation of committee to draft safety standards for goalposts.

Following a number of deaths of children involving temporary goalposts, Minister for Trade and Commerce Michael Adhern (Tuesday 19th April 2005) announced the formation of The National Standards Authority of Ireland (NSAI) Committee on Goalpost safety.

Sadly 4 children in Ireland have been killed in recent years and many more injured by unsafe goalposts. This is not a sole Irish experience, 13 children have been killed in Britain in recent years, more than twenty children have been killed in America and deaths have also been recorded in Australia and Malta.

A Football Goalpost Killed My Son

Mum relives son's death

by ROB SINGH

*rob.singh@
thisisessex.co.uk*

THE mother of a Witham boy who died in a goalpost accident has been devastated by the death of a 10-year-old Irish boy in carbon-copy circumstances.

Lee Myles, 10, of Dundalk, Ireland, was playing with a group of children as he waited to watch his father in a local league game when a goalpost fell and hit him on Sunday.

He was rushed to hospital in Navan, Co Meath, with serious head injuries but died a short time later.

Brenda Smith, of Tees Close, whose 11-year-old son, Jonathan, died in 1991 in similar circumstances, has campaigned tirelessly, along with the Football Association, for legislation to be implemented to make sure goalposts are secure and safeguard children's safety.

Jonathan was killed after a set of insecure goalposts made of metal tubing collapsed on him.

The FA say: "Under no circumstances should children use the goalposts as gymnastic equipment, and goalposts should not be used at all, unless they are in good condition, securely anchored to the ground and are stable."

Adrin Cooper, of the FA, said there were British Standard measures for goalposts, which were in place. It was making sure they were known by all national bodies.

He said: "We are very close to circulating comprehensive documents for pitches and pitch providers, which basically outline the rights and responsibilities for goalpost safety."

I was again contacted by the media; it seems a shame that the only time I can get publicity for the campaign is when a child has lost its life. This time a freelance reporter called Adam Fresco contacted me for a story which I willingly gave. It appeared on the front page of The Time newspaper. Following on from this I had interviews with BBC News, Essex News, Radio 5 Live, Anglia News and. This can only be good to get my point across to warn parents, carers and schools etc of the dangers of unsafe goalposts.

A Football Goalpost Killed My Son

Children killed by collapsing goalposts

By Adam Fresco

THE FOOTBALL Association is planning a £1 million initiative to replace unsafe portable goalposts that have been responsible for causing the deaths of dozens of children across the world, *The Times* has learnt.

The FA has sent more than a million leaflets to schools and sports clubs warning them that home-made posts should not be used as they "have been the cause of a number of deaths and injuries".

Thirteen children have been killed in recent years and thousands more injured by unsecured goalposts in Britain. More than 20 children have been killed in America by falling posts and crossbars, and others have died in Australia, Ireland and Malta.

The British Standards Institution has warned goalpost manufacturers that if their goals do not pass strict tests of strength and stability then they will not be able to display its BSI logo. It is hoped that the threat, backed by the FA and the Department of Culture, Media and Sport, will lead to companies improving their equipment.

Brenda Smith, whose son, Jonathan, died aged 11 in 1991 when a goal fell on him, has been a leading campaigner to ensure that portable posts are made secure. Mrs Smith said: "My constant concern is that the 'man down the street' will continue to make home-made goalposts and take no notice of the safety guidelines.

"I would urge all parents to check goalposts before their child plays, to make sure they are safe and secure and to prevent any further needless accidents."

Goals are often freestanding and there is no legal obligation to secure them to the ground, so when children swing on them they come crashing down.

A recent FA survey found that 42 per cent of mini-soccer goals, 50 per cent of five-a-side goals and 22 per cent of junior goals failed stability tests. A set of full-size metal posts blew over during an under-12s game this year at a professional football club.

Legislation will be needed to make sure that unsecured portable posts are banned. Alex Stone, from the FA, said: "We have put out leaflets, but it is for the Government to put forward legislation. Some local authorities are continuing to use wooden posts, which we have found are the most dangerous."

A Football Goalpost Killed My Son

Soccer team scores with new goalposts

FOOTBALLERS on
school team have n
excuse for missing th
target – thanks to a
Essex mum's 14-year pla
ground safety campaign.
Gleaming new goalpos
at Alresford Primary wei
partly paid for with fun
from the Sports Found
tion, lobbied for by Wit
am woman Brenda Smit
whose son Jonathan di
when insecure posts cc
lapsed on him in 1991.
The school's part-tin
coach, Mike Deal, appli
to the Football Associ
tion-funded charity aft
reading in the Evenir
Gazette last year how tl
money had been set asid
Travel firm ROL the
matched its £220 don
tion.
Mr Deal said: "I want t
thank the Football Fou
dation, ROL Travel ar
your paper for making t
aware that there are pe
ple out there workir
hard to enable children
play sport safely."

On target for success – the Alresford Primary School football team with the new goalposts.

Good news at last a school has new goalposts with funds from the Football Foundation.

When I started to write my book first book, I did it mainly for myself and hopefully to help other families, with my experience of bringing up a child with complex special needs.

Little did I realize the impact it would have when I included in my book, the traumas and the fight that I had on my hands for the next 17 years, after losing my darling son Jonathan in a goalpost accident.

Starting the goalpost campaign got rid of my anger and frustration from the needless deaths that I had found out had happened.

After my last meeting on the 18th February 2008 with the Football Association at Soho Square in London, I decided that I should catalogue my campaign and have it printed so that the safety

A Football Goalpost Killed My Son

message about unsafe goalposts could reach the rest of the world, which I never thought possible.

Without my input The Football Association would not have:

1. Commissioned the goalpost survey to ascertain the percentage of unsafe goalposts.

2. Distributed leaflets/posters which highlight: Check it! Secure it! Test! Respect it!
3. Introduced a rolling program of funding, jointly with the Football foundation to renew all unsafe goalposts.

I can only thank them for helping me to produce a safer game of football, which I love to watch, and give parents and cares the peace of mind and reassurance when their children play football.

VICTIM: Craig died on his holidays
VICTIM: Posts toppled on Sophia
VICTIM: Mobile goal trapped Paul   TRAGIC: Jonathan Smith with the goal that killed him in the background   VICTIM: Jack's death sparked action

The goalposts in the background are not the ones that killed Jonathan as stated in the photo.

A Football Goalpost Killed My Son

I dedicate this book to all the children above who have all lost there lives from unsafe goalposts, also to many more children and adults around the world.

I only hope now that the Government and the Football Association get together to bring in legislation, so that my campaign for the past seventeen years has not been in vain. Also, that no other person in the world has to suffer the trauma and heartache that my family and others have.

My message is to think before you play football of the possible dangers of unsafe goalposts.

Check it!

Secure it!

Test it!

Respect it!   www.TheFA.com

www.ingramcontent.com/pod-product-compliance
Lightning Source LLC
Chambersburg PA
CBHW031933080426
42734CB00007B/670